D0839210

BOOK ANALYSIS

Written by Natalia Torres Behar
Translated by Emma Hanna

Midnight's Children
BY SALMAN RUSHDIE

Bright
≡Summaries.com

SALMAN RUSHDIE

BRITISH INDIAN WRITER

- **Born in Bombay (now Mumbai) in 1947.**
- **Literary awards:**
  - Man Booker Prize, 1981 (for *Midnight's Children*)
  - Hans Christian Andersen Literature Award, 2014
  - PEN Pinter Prize, 2014
- **Notable honours:**
  - Knight Bachelor of the Order of the British Empire, 2007
  - Honorary Professorship at the Massachusetts Institute of Technology
  - Fellow of the Royal Society of Literature
- **Notable works:**
  - *Midnight's Children* (1981), novel
  - *The Satanic Verses* (1988), novel
  - *Haroun and the Sea of Stories* (1990), novel
  - *Shalimar the Clown* (2005), novel

Ahmed Salman Rushdie was born in Bombay on 19 June 1947, two months before the end of British colonialism in India. He grew up in a middle-class Muslim family of Kashmiri descent, although his father was not religious. At home, his family spoke both English, the language of the cultural elite in newly independent India, and Urdu, the national language of Pakistan and one of the 22 official languages of India.

Rushdie left his homeland in 1961, at the age of 14, to study in the UK, where he attended Rugby School, one of the most prestigious boarding schools in the country. He went on to study history at King's College, University of Cambridge, and graduated in 1968. During this time, Rushdie specialised in Muslim history and religion, which provided him with the theoretical knowledge which would later inform his political ideology and literary style. His writing also draws heavily on Indian history, and on the distinctive blend of indigenous beliefs and mythology and Western influences introduced during the colonial era which has shaped the country's modern identity.

Rushdie's literary career began in 1975 with the publication of *Grimus*, a novel which blends fantasy with elements of science fiction. Although this debut effort was not particularly successful, his literary career took off in 1981 with the publication of his next novel, *Midnight's Children*, which catapulted Rushdie to international fame. This novel is now considered one of the most significant works of fiction of the 20th century, and a milestone in English-language Indian literature. It earned Rushdie a number of awards, including the 1981 Man Booker Prize, the UK's most prestigious literary award. When the novel was first published, it proved somewhat controversial in India due to the inclusion of remarks which were perceived as derogatory towards then-Prime Minister Indira Gandhi (Indian stateswoman, 1917-1984); however, an even greater controversy erupted in 1988 with the publication of Rushdie's fourth novel, *The Satanic Verses*. Due to the novel's allegedly irreverent depiction of the Prophet Muhammad, it was deemed blasphemous and denounced throughout the Muslim world.

THE SATANIC VERSES

When *The Satanic Verses* was published in the United Kingdom, it sparked intense controversy which led to the novel being banned and publicly burned in a number of Muslim countries; in 1989, Ayatollah Ruhollah Khomeini (Iranian religious leader and politician, 1902-1989) even issued a religious edict known as a *fatwā* against Rushdie, accusing the novel of committing blasphemy against Islam and its author of apostasy. This edict imposed a death sentence on the writer – with a bounty of $3 million being placed on his head – and on any person associated with the publication of the book. As a result, the translator of the Japanese version of the novel was murdered, and the translator of the Italian version and the novel's Norwegian publisher were both seriously injured in assassination attempts. Rushdie was placed under police protection and largely withdrew from the public eye, and although Iran is no longer actively calling for his execution, a *fatwā* can only be revoked by the person who issued it, namely Khomeini, who died in 1989 without retracting it. Consequently, there are a number of fundamentalist groups who still consider the *fatwā* to be valid, although they are not supported by the Iranian government.

MIDNIGHT'S CHILDREN

A BLEND OF FANTASY, HISTORY AND HUMANITY

- **Genre:** novel
- **Reference edition:** Rushdie, S. (2008) *Midnight's Children*. London: Vintage.
- **1st edition:** 1981
- **Themes:** the individual vs. the collective, creation, destruction, preservation, the reliability of the narrator

Midnight's Children was first published in 1981. It is Salman Rushdie's second novel, and was the book that first propelled him to widespread critical and popular renown. The story is narrated by its protagonist, Saleem Sinai, who was born on 15 August 1947 – the very same day that India gained its independence from the British Empire. Saleem feels profoundly connected to his homeland, and his life echoes and is impacted by the transition and the way the political situation in India changes over time. *Midnight's Children* tells the story of one man and his family, but it is also the portrait of a generation and a culture, and combines history, fantasy and humanity in a dynamic, daring manner to create a truly astonishing novel.

SUMMARY

Midnight's Children is narrated by its protagonist, Saleem Sinai, who begins his story by telling the reader that he was born at midnight on 15 August 1947, at the exact moment when India gained its independence from the British Empire. This moment bound the destinies of Saleem and his country inextricably together; however, nearly 30 years later, his body has been left ravaged by the vicissitudes of history, which has led him to believe that his time is running out and that his death is imminent. For this reason, he decides to tell his story as quickly as he can: "In short, I am literally disintegrating, slowly for the moment, although there are signs of acceleration. [...] This is why I have resolved to confide in paper, before I forget. (We are a nation of forgetters.)" (p. 43). Padma, his fiancée and loyal companion, listens to his story patiently, although she also makes occasional interjections.

BOOK ONE: 1915-1947

Saleem's story begins in 1915, 32 years before he is born, when his grandfather Aadam Aziz returns to his hometown in Kashmir after studying medicine abroad and begins treating Naseem, who later becomes his wife. Aadam spends three years checking up on his patient, who is always covered by a sheet with a hole cut in it so that he can only see the part of her body that he needs to examine. The doctor gradually falls in love with the resulting collage-like mental image that he develops of his patient, and the first time he sees her without the sheet between them is in 1918, just after the end of the First World War, on their wedding day.

The young couple move to Agra and have five children together: Alia, Mumtaz, Emerald, Mustapha and Hanif. Aadam becomes a follower of the anti-Partitionist cause championed by the activist Mian Abdullah, known as "the Hummingbird", who is also the chairman of the Free Islam Convocation. When the Hummingbird is assassinated, Aadam takes in his assistant Nadir Khan, who survived the attack, against the wishes of his wife. While Khan is hiding from his enemies in the Aziz family's house, he falls in love with Mumtaz and marries her. However, Mumtaz falls gravely ill after they have been married for two years, and when her father examines her, he realises that she is still a virgin. Her youngest sister, Emerald, reacts to this revelation – which is seen as an affront to the family's honour – by confessing to Major Zulfikar (an officer in the Pakistani army whom she later marries) that her family has been sheltering Khan. The young man is forced to flee the Aziz family home, but leaves a note declaring that he is divorcing Mumtaz. She is then free to marry Ahmed Sinai, a young businessman who had previously courted her sister Alia.

At her husband's suggestion, Mumtaz changes her name to Amina and moves to New Delhi with him. Tensions between the city's Hindu and Muslim populations are mounting on a daily basis, and business owners of Muslim descent are targeted by groups like the Ravana gang, who threaten to burn down factories, shops and warehouses owned by Muslims unless they are paid off. Meanwhile, any Hindus who are found in the city's Muslim neighbourhoods, known as *muhallas*, run the risk of being lynched. One day, Amina decides to save Lifafa Das, a Hindu who has brought his peepshow into the neighbourhood, from the mob that is threatening to lynch him, even though she is pregnant at the time. In exchange, the young man makes her an appointment with his cousin, Shri Ramram Seth, a renowned seer who will be able to predict her son's future. Unbeknownst to her husband, Amina goes to the Old Fort to meet the seer, who gives her a prophecy:

> "A son [...] who will never be older than his motherland – neither older nor younger. [...] There will be two heads – but you shall see only one – there will be knees and a nose, a nose and knees. [...] Newspaper praises him, two mothers raise him! [...] He will have sons without having sons! He will be old before he is old! And he will die before he is dead." (pp. 114-115)

After Ahmed's factory is attacked by the Ravana gang, the couple decide to move to Bombay. On the same day, an announcement is made that the Partition of India will take place 70 days later. The couple buy one of the four houses on Methwold

Estate, a property owned by an Englishman called William Methwold who is hoping to return to England in light of the current political situation. During their time there, they meet Wee Willie Winkie, a poor man who entertains the families living on the Estate with his accordion, and his wife Vanita, who is also pregnant – but with Methwold's child. Shortly afterwards, both women go into labour and give birth to a child at exactly midnight on 15 August, putting them in the running for the prize offered by the *Times of India* for any mother who gives birth at the exact moment that the new nation is born. However, the attending midwife, Mary Pereira, switches the babies, meaning that the child who should have been destined for a life of privilege and riches is instead condemned to a life of poverty, and vice versa. Although Mary initially thinks that this act will win the respect of her lover, a radical socialist called Joseph D'Costa, she is soon consumed by remorse. She therefore seeks Amina out and asks for a job as Saleem's nanny, as a way of atoning for her actions.

BOOK TWO: 1947-1965

Saleem Sinai is born with a long nose and bright blue eyes like his grandfather. Meanwhile, Wee Willie Winkie's son, who is called Shiva after the Hindu god of procreation and destruction, has dangerously strong knees and silently blames himself for his father's decline. As a result, he lives in a state of constant simmering anger. Meanwhile, life goes on in the Sinai household, even as the country experiences shocks and upheaval like the assassination of Mahatma Gandhi (Indian political activist, 1869-1948). In 1948, Amina gives birth to a second child: a daughter who is universally known as the "Brass Monkey" because of her thick red-gold hair, and who quickly learns that the key to ensuring that other people pay attention to her is to make a great deal of noise.

As Saleem grows up, it becomes clear that everyone expects something from him. Things only escalate when he starts school, where the other children make fun of him because of his massive nose, which is always running, and call him names like "Pinocchio", "Cucumber-nose" and "Goo-face". Saleem develops the habit of seeking refuge in the laundry basket, where he hides among the clothes and sheets and is finally able to forget about the outside world – and even about his elephantine nose, which could almost belong to the Hindu elephant-god Ganesh. However, one day Amina comes into the bathroom while he is hiding in the laundry basket, and he overhears her crying and murmuring the name of her former husband, Nadir Khan. When she gets undressed and goes to place her clothes in the laundry basket, she realises that her son has been eavesdropping on her, and punishes him by forbidding him to speak for the next day. During this time, Saleem realises for the first time that he can hear voices in his mind, just like the prophecy foretold: "Washing will hide him – voices will guide him!" (*ibid*.). However, his parents do not believe him and he is punished for making up stories.

Saleem soon realises that he also has the gift of telepathy, but instead of using this ability in a noble way, for example by improving the quality of life of India's impoverished citizens, he hides his talent so that he can read the minds of film stars, cricket players and even the Prime Minister. When Saleem turns ten, he starts hearing the voices of the other children who, like him, were born at around midnight on the day India became an independent country. At first, there were 1001 of them, but by the time Saleem reaches his tenth birthday, only 581 of the children are still alive, as the others have died of malnutrition, illness and the general hardships of their everyday lives. Saleem's gift means that he is the only one who is aware of the existence of these "midnight children", and he discovers that each of them has a power that may even be a hindrance to them: one of them is so beautiful that she blinds anyone who looks at her, while another can enter a mirror and emerge from any other reflective surface. Interestingly, the closer to midnight the children were born, the stronger their gifts. Those with the strongest gifts include Parvati-the-witch, who can perform real magic, and Shiva, whose gift for fighting is evidenced by his powerful knees. Saleem discovers that his gift is the most powerful of all: he has the ability to read other people's thoughts and emotions. He therefore decides to create the "Midnight Children's Conference", a means of gathering all the children together so that they can talk to each other. Shiva and Saleem meet for the first time at one of these conferences, and become rivals when they both try to assume the mantle of the group's leader.

Not long afterwards, Saleem gets into a fight with his classmates during a school dance and loses part of his middle finger. He is taken to hospital, where a blood test reveals that he is not his parents' biological son. They then send him to live with his uncle Hanif and his wife Pia until the situation calms down, and from that moment on, Saleem's life begins to unravel: he is no longer seen as the firstborn son who was ushered proudly into the family home, but as a source of dishonour and confusion.

Meanwhile, tensions begin to brew between the members of the Midnight Children's Conference due to their cultural and religious differences, as the children have inherited many of their parents' prejudices. Saleem tries to hold the group together: "Do not let this happen! Do not permit the endless duality of masses-and-classes, capital-and-labour, them-and-us to come between us! [...] for only by being other, by being new, can we fulfil the promise of our birth!" (p. 354). However, his idealism clashes with the harsh reality represented by Shiva, whose life of hardship has led him to see the world as a dichotomy between rich and poor, left and right. As a result, their paths eventually diverge.

After Uncle Hanif commits suicide, the family all gathers together in Bombay, and Mary Pereira takes advantage of this reunion to reveal the truth at last. Ahmed, who is now an alcoholic and is growing weaker by the day, takes reprisals against Amina and sends her and her two children to Pakistan to live with Saleem's aunt Emerald. Saleem is somewhat relieved by this outcome, as this will put some distance between Shiva and himself, and he is afraid that Shiva will discover Mary Pereira's secret and the fact that he was the real "rich kid". During their time in Pakistan, he and his family help General Zulfikar to mount a coup d'état against the Pakistani government.

Four years later, in 1962, the family is forced to return to Bombay after Ahmed has a heart attack. At around the same time, India declares war on China, the Midnight Children's

Conference disbands and Saleem's nose becomes so congested that he requires surgery. He loses his telepathic powers as a result, but his sense of smell becomes so acute that he can sense other people's emotions. After India is defeated, the entire family returns to Pakistan, where the Brass Monkey adopts the stage name Jamila Singer and embarks on a musical career. The distance between himself and Shiva makes Saleem feel more at ease, although he always feels like a stranger in a foreign land because of the increasingly strict Muslim laws in Pakistan.

In 1965, war breaks out between Pakistan and India, with devastating consequences for Saleem's family: on 22 September of that year, his grandmother Naseem, Pia, Amina and the unborn child she is carrying, Ahmed and Alia are all killed in an airstrike. Only Jamila and Saleem survive, but Saleem is struck by a silver spittoon inlaid with lapis lazuli which had belonged to his grandfather, and loses his memory. However, this allows him to regain his former innocence and purity.

BOOK THREE: 1970-1978

Saleem's memory loss reduces him to an almost animalistic state – more specifically, he seems more dog than human thanks to his keen sense of smell, which leads the Pakistani army to start using him as a bloodhound to hunt down Indians. Although he has no real idea of what is happening or how he ended up in this situation, this conflict has arisen because India is supporting Bangladeshi efforts to gain independence from Pakistan. In 1971, Saleem travels to Dhaka with 60 000 Pakistani soldiers in search of Sheikh Mujib. As they enter the city, Saleem bears witness to all kinds of atrocities, including rapes, murders and thefts, but he never questions the orders he is given and goes into the Sundarbans forest with the rest of his platoon. When they realise that Mujib is nowhere to be found, they break off from the main group and get lost in the forest, where Saleem is bitten by a snake. However, he is saved by its venom, as it brings all of his memories rushing back – although he is still unable to remember his name. After escaping and returning to Dhaka, Saleem meets Parvati-the witch, who tells him his name and helps him to return to India by smuggling him across the border in a wicker basket. At this time, he discovers that the Indian army is being led by Shiva, and that Indira Gandhi has the support of two thirds of the National Assembly.

Saleem lives with Parvati-the-witch and a snake charmer called Picture Singh in the magicians' ghetto, which is dominated by Communists. Parvati-the-witch uses her spells to restore the hair that Saleem lost as a child, erase his birthmarks and strengthen his legs, but she wants him to become her lover in exchange. For Saleem, this is an impossible request, as he sees his sister's face every time he looks at her. After Saleem rejects her by faking impotence, her face becomes fixed in a constant pout which cannot be dispelled by any form of magic.

Parvati-the-witch later contacts Shiva, who is lauded as India's most highly decorated war hero upon his arrival in the magician's ghetto. He and Parvati-the-witch become lovers, but their relationship comes to an abrupt end, and Parvati-the-witch is left pregnant and alone. In 1975, Saleem marries her, and she adopts the name Laylah Sinai (in accordance with Muslim tradition). Saleem raises the child as his own son, and names him Aadam. Instead of a large nose, the baby has enormous ears which flap up and down and from side to side, giving his head an elephantine appearance like Ganesh's. However, he never speaks, perhaps because his large ears are so sensitive that they allow him to hear too much. The timing of his birth is also significant: Laylah spends 13 days in labour, which corresponds exactly to the length of time that it took for Indira Gandhi to place the country in a state of emergency, which lasted for two years during which the press was heavily censored and political opposition was suppressed.

As the Prime Minister tries to influence the course of history by adopting slogans such as "India is Indira and Indira is India" (p. 587), her destiny becomes increasingly entwined with Saleem's. The government learns of the existence of the Midnight Children's Conference and invades the magicians' ghetto, and the soldiers are instructed to gun down women, children and Communists indiscriminately. Laylah and Saleem are separated by the army and Aadam is left abandoned in their home, as his parents are unable to rescue him. At that moment, Shiva appears on the scene, and it is revealed that he had his own sinister motives for helping to organise the attack on the ghetto, during which Laylah is killed.

The government begins to fear that the midnight children could pass on their powers to their offspring, and in January 1977 Indira Gandhi embarks on a campaign to sterilise them all, scheduling 23 vasectomies and hysterectomies to be performed per day. This sterilisation process not only prevents the midnight children from reproducing, but also takes away their magical abilities, and with them, their hope. However, Indira Gandhi loses the elections, and her political career enters a downward spiral.

The surviving midnight children are released, including Saleem, who is reunited with his son Aadam, who was being looked after by Picture Singh. The family decides to return to Bombay, where Saleem meets a woman called Padma who works at a chutney factory owned by Mary Pereira, the only one of Saleem's mother figures left alive. Saleem gains a sense of closure after being reunited with Mary, and the narrative begins to focus less on the past and more on the present, with Saleem deciding to marry Padma, before looking to the future, when Saleem dies on his 31st birthday – in other words, on the 31st anniversary of India's independence – by exploding into 6 million particles of dust. The novel ends with a prophecy by the narrator:

> "Yes, they will trample me underfoot, [...] reducing me to specks of voiceless dust, just as, all in good time, they will trample my son who is not my son, and his son who will not be his, and his who will not be his, until the thousand and first generation, [...] because it is the privilege and the curse of midnight's children to be both masters and victims of their times" (p. 647)

CHARACTER STUDY

SALEEM SINAI

Saleem is the protagonist and narrator of *Midnight's Children*. He was born at midnight on 15 August 1947, at the exact moment that India became an independent country. He was switched at birth with another child who was born at the same time as him, which means that Saleem leads a life of luxury while the other boy is doomed to the impoverished life of an orphan. At the age of nine, Saleem discovers that he is a telepath, and his large cucumber-like nose also endows him with an exceptionally acute sense of smell. These two gifts allow him to find many of the other "midnight children" who, like him, were born at around midnight on the day India became independent, and who therefore have supernatural powers. Together, they form the Midnight Children's Conference.

The main events that shape Saleem's life are closely linked to the history of India, meaning that his life is marked by upheaval and loss. By the time he turns 30, he feels as though he could die at any moment, because his body is about to shatter into 6 million dust particles, and he therefore rushes to finish telling his life story.

PADMA MANGROLI

Padma is Saleem's carer, and later becomes his fiancée. She has strong, hairy forearms and a cheerful, energetic disposition. She is a source of comfort to Saleem in his last days, because she remains by his side throughout this time, even though his strength is failing and he cannot do much for her. Like the reader, Padma listens to Saleem as he tells his life story over the course of the novel, but she also interrupts him any time she has a question or if she disagrees with him about something, and when Saleem starts to lose his focus, Padma nudges him back on track. Padma plays two main roles in the novel: firstly, she serves as Saleem's foil, as she is much less idealistic and quixotic than him, and secondly, she acts as a narrative device. Rushdie's prose is often jumbled and disorienting, which can make it difficult to understand at times. However, Padma is able to act as a kind of mouthpiece for the reader, addressing the narrator directly and asking him the questions that the reader may also be wondering about, as well as reminding him to focus on the central narrative thread. In this way, the characters of Saleem and Padma complement each other to create a more balanced narrative.

SHIVA

This character is named after the Indian god of procreation and destruction. He was born at midnight on 15 August 1947, the day India became independent. He was born at the same time as Saleem, but the babies were switched by Mary Pereira, and Shiva (the biological son of Amina and Ahmed) was condemned to a life of poverty with Wee Willie Winkie, who is neither his nor Saleem's biological father. Unlike Saleem, who is timid and cautious, Shiva grows up feeling responsible for his father's gradual decline, and is a born fighter, as evidenced by his impressively large knees, which make him a hero of the Indo-Pakistani Wars.

Shiva represents the lower, underprivileged classes of Indian society, and unlike Saleem, he finds it very difficult to believe that his actions will lead to any kind of positive change, particularly as one of the midnight children. From his humble beginnings as a member of one of Bombay's street gangs, Shiva rises to become a highly decorated war hero, which also gives him the chance to seduce many of the most prominent women in Indian high society before leaving them pregnant and alone, and he never takes responsibility for any of his children. Shiva eventually betrays the midnight children, who are considered a political threat by Indira Gandhi and are sterilised. As a result, they lose their powers, but this also leads to Shiva's downfall.

PARVATI-THE-WITCH

Like Shiva and Saleem, Parvati-the-witch was one of the children born at the moment that India gained independence. She joins the Midnight Children's Conference at a young age, and even in those early days she always sides with Saleem. Years later, when she finds him in Dhaka during the war with Pakistan, Parvati helps him to remember his name and smuggles him across the border to India in a wicker basket.

Although Parvati can perform real spells and witchcraft, she never manages to make Saleem fall in love with her; instead, she embarks on a relationship with Shiva, who abandons her after getting her pregnant. When Saleem learns of this situation, he marries her and raises her son, Aadam, as his own, even after she dies in the skirmishes that are started in the magicians' ghetto by Shiva and Indira Gandhi. Interestingly, in Hindu mythology the god Shiva's consort is called Parvati.

INDIRA GANDHI

Indira Gandhi was the Prime Minister of India from 1966 to 1977 and again from 1980 to 1984, when she was assassinated. Her popularity surged in 1971 during the Indo-Pakistani War, which eventually resulted in the country of Bangladesh being created. However, in the following years she faced increasing opposition due to allegations of electoral fraud, and she eventually declared a nationwide state of emergency during which personal freedoms and freedom of expression were heavily curtailed. Although Gandhi does not appear in person until Book

Three, the novel makes frequent references to a mysterious figure known as "the Widow" who will eventually destroy the midnight children, and who is later revealed to be Indira Gandhi. Her appearance in the novel is brief but memorable, as she takes advantage of Shiva's betrayal to build sterilisation camps and destroy the magicians' ghetto. These actions represent India's decision to reject a more hopeful, promising future and sink back into darkness.

ANALYSIS

FORM

Structure

Midnight's Children comprises three sections, or books, which are unnamed. The novel displays two of the most characteristic features of Salman Rushdie's writing: a non-linear timeline and a story which blends reality and fantasy and is recounted by a possibly unreliable narrator.

Since the narrator's main goal is to tell his life story, the novel is presented as a collection of his memories, and it spans a period of 46 years (15 of which the narrator did not experience, as he had not yet been born). The entire story is told in the first person, using a writing style known as stream of consciousness which aims to realistically mimic the narrator's flow of speech, and the narration constantly jumps back to the present in almost every chapter. Both of these characteristics remind the reader that this story is a work in progress which the protagonist is telling us in real time, and this idea is further reinforced through Padma's constant interruptions, for example when she "[bullies Saleem] back into the world of linear narrative, the universe of what-happened-next" (p. 44), or when the narrator imagines Padma telling him to start the story at the beginning.

The novel's focus is somewhat jumbled and shifts between the past and the present because the protagonist can sense his own death approaching and knows that his time is running out, but also feels the pressure not to leave out a single detail, which can lead to chronological inconsistencies and some unrealistic scenes. As we have already mentioned, Rushdie frequently writes from a subjective perspective which is no less valid for being less than entirely factual, and reality and fantasy work together and complement each other in *Midnight's Children*, endowing the text with additional layers of meaning.

Language and style: Rushdie and magical realism

Throughout the novel, Rushdie uses an extremely wide variety of literary styles and techniques to tell the stories of both Saleem's life and the history of India, his native country. Each chapter of the novel can stand on its own, and the novel combines diverse elements including humour, political commentary, humanity, desperation, ambition, violence, history and magic. Rushdie therefore adopts a writing style which disregards fixed grammatical rules in order to fully convey the richness of these themes and to rise to the challenge he has set for himself: to write a novel as diverse and wide-ranging as India itself, creating a veritable mosaic of cultural contrasts.

The border between reality and fantasy becomes nothing more than an illusion in Rushdie's writing; reality is merely a matter of perspective, and the writer therefore has the power to create their own reality. As such, the universe they build may not be entirely aligned with their readers' worldviews; for example, the novel includes a number of fantastic elements which are reminiscent of the genre of magical realism, which originated in Latin American. This style is chiefly associated with the works of the Colombian writer Gabriel García Márquez (1927-2014), in which supernatural elements frequently affect the characters' lives. However, these fantastic occurrences are not presented as anything out of the ordinary, but merely as a part of everyday life. Similarly, magic is a vital part of Saleem's life, and by extension of life in India as a whole. His descriptions of these supernatural elements, and therefore the entire story, could be interpreted as true or false, depending on how the reader chooses to view them. In *Midnight's Children*, writing becomes a game in which neither the hero nor the writer wields absolute power.

THEMES

The individual vs. the collective

Saleem Sinai was born at midnight on the day India became an independent nation, and his destiny is inextricably linked to that of his country. A closer analysis of the novel reveals that the major events of Saleem's life occur on the same dates as important milestones in Indian history: for example, the Midnight Children's Conference collapses completely on the same day that the Chinese army sweeps down from the Himalayas and crushes the forces mustered by the Indian *fauj*. Similarly, many historical events have a direct impact on the lives of Saleem and his family members, such as the Indo-Pakistani War of 1965, which Saleem believes to have broken out for the express purpose of wiping out his family line. The question of whether or not all the complexities of a nation with as much linguistic, cultural and religious diversity as India can be contained within a single person is one of the main sources of tension within the novel, as can be seen at the end when the main character literally disintegrates, mirroring the fragmentation of India following the Partition.

Nevertheless, there are also some differences between Saleem and his country. India, like Pakistan (and later Bangladesh), is still trying to define its identity in terms of language, religious beliefs and political alignment. However, Saleem's telepathic powers allow him to transcend linguistic, religious and cultural barriers, and his heritage is full of contradictions: he is half English, is from an impoverished family, had a comfortable upbringing in an environment where he was exposed to a variety of religions and has roots in both the East and the West. These traits, among others, reflect the immense diversity of India, and show that it would be impossible to identify any one aspect of its history, or any one individual, as "purely Indian":

> "Who what am I? My answer: I am the sum total of everything that went before me, of all I have been seen done, of everything done-to-me. [...] Nor am I particularly exceptional in this matter; each 'I', every one of the now-six-hundred-million-plus of us, contains a similar multitude." (p. 535)

Although this quote shows that the individual and the collective are inextricably connected – an idea which is reinforced by the image of Saleem disintegrating into particles of dust, each of which is intended to represent one of the inhabitants of India, which had a population of around 600 million at the time the novel was written – the novel also shows that this inevitably leads to differences of opinion, as demonstrated by events such as the Partition and the Indo-Pakistani Wars, among others.

The Midnight Children's Conference could be considered one of Saleem's attempts to construct a pluralist system for the fledgling nation to adopt, wherein each child's differences and powers would make the group more powerful instead of leaving it divided. However, as reflected by the history of India itself, this model fails. The children begin to cluster together with those who share their native language and place of origin, and older generations pass their own prejudices and hatred down to their children, turning them against each other and splitting the group apart. In some ways, this is representative of the rift that violence and intolerance created between the people of India and Pakistan, which was heavily felt in those days and remains a constant presence even today. Both countries are still in the process of defining their religious and cultural identities as a result of the Partition.

Creation, destruction and preservation

The novel's examination of the themes of creation, destruction and preservation has many echoes of Hindu mythology, in which Brahma, Vishnu and Shiva (the trinity of gods who are generally considered the most powerful in the Hindu belief system) each personify one of these elements. Given that Shiva is the incarnation of destruction (while Brahma embodies creation and Vishnu represents preservation), it is perhaps unsurprising that the character named after him is also a martially gifted force of destruction. His rivalry with Saleem spans most of the novel, beginning when they are switched at birth, and develops in parallel with the novel's examination of these three themes.

Shiva proves his strength and martial prowess by rising through the ranks of the Indian army during the Indo-Pakistani War, and later lives up to his namesake's reputation by betraying the midnight children and leading Indira Gandhi to set up camps where they can be forcibly sterilised, thus destroying their powers. However, the destruction wrought by the god Shiva is believed to be for the purpose of allowing new creation to spring forth, and Shiva also creates life throughout the novel: he fights for his own survival from the moment he is born, and during the war he has children with the daughters of the richest men in India, perhaps in defiance of his humble origins.

The concept of preservation is chiefly addressed through the theme of legacy. Shiva's plans to utterly destroy the midnight children are foiled because, unbeknownst to him, he is the biological father of Aadam, whom Saleem raises as his own son. This fulfils the prophecy that Amina's child will have sons without having sons, and that his family line will continue for a thousand and one generations, thus creating a legacy which preserves the spirit of India itself and transcends the life of any one individual.

The reliability of the narrator

Midnight's Children is the narrator's last, desperate attempt to tell the story of his life and all the other lives and events that have intersected with it, as he can feel his death approaching at a rapid pace. Even though Saleem is the story's narrator as well as its protagonist, he is not omniscient and he cannot control the narrative; instead, the reader (who is represented within the novel by Padma) must implicitly agree to accept the protagonist's perspective of the events he describes as true, while also accepting the possibility that Saleem is altering the story to make it align more closely with his own worldview, or to place himself in the central role within it by rewriting the years he lived through. Although the history of

India is closely linked to the story of Saleem and his family, a close examination of the novel reveals a number of inconsistencies and errors: for example, the date of Mahatma Gandhi's death is incorrect. Furthermore, many of the events described in the novel are utterly unrealistic, such as the scene in which Saleem's grandmother, the Reverend Mother, starts swelling up like a balloon because of the words she has left unsaid after taking a vow of silence, and when his father Ahmed starts suffering from an illness which causes his skin to start turning whiter as he gets richer (which is a metaphor for Europeanisation). However, as Saleem says, reality is a matter of perspective, and he is more interested in telling a story that will satisfy him, even when he is no longer present, than in creating an objective narrative. The story's verisimilitude is therefore relegated to a role of secondary importance, and it is left up to the reader, who is reminded that history is malleable and is inevitably shaped by the person who writes it, to fill in the blanks and read between the lines.

According to Rafael Martínez Bernardo, "Rushdie emphasises the role the novelist plays in shaping this subjective, fragmented perception of reality.

But if the novelist must distance themselves from the realist tradition, then the reader must do the same, and break the habit of expecting fiction to be lifelike"[1] (Martínez, 1991: 28). A novel like *Midnight's Children* therefore requires the reader to interpret the text and form their own perspective.

---

1. This quotation has been translated by BrightSummaries.com.

FURTHER REFLECTION

SOME QUESTIONS TO THINK ABOUT...

- In your opinion, what do the midnight children symbolise?
- What role does religion play in the novel?
- To what extent is Saleem a reliable narrator?
- What is the significance of Padma's role in the novel?
- Why do you think Saleem adopted Parvati-the-witch's son? What was the significance of this gesture?
- What do the nose and knees represent in this novel?
- What does the sterilisation of the midnight children represent for the future of India?
- What role do women play in the novel?
- Who is Saleem telling his life story to? Himself? Padma? The reader?
- In what way does the novel provide a timeline of the early decades of the history of India as an independent republic?

We want to hear from you!
Leave a comment on your online library
and share your favourite books on social media!

FURTHER READING

REFERENCE EDITION

- Rushdie, S. (2008) *Midnight's Children*. London: Vintage.

REFERENCE STUDIES

- Gurnah, A. (2007) Themes and Structures in Midnight's Children. *The Cambridge Companion to Salman Rushdie*. Cambridge: Cambridge University Press. pp. 91-108.

- Martínez Bernardo, R. (1991) *Salman Rushdie, recreador de la historia mágica y mítica*. Salamanca: University of Salamanca.

- Reynolds, M. and Noakes, J. (2003) *Salman Rushdie: The Essential Guide*. London: Vintage.

RECOMMENDED READING

- Gurnah, A. (2007) *The Cambridge Companion to Salman Rushdie*. Cambridge: Cambridge University Press.

ADAPTATIONS

- *Midnight's Children.* (2012) [Film]. Deepa Mehta. Dir. Canada/UK: Mongrel.

www.brightsummaries.com

Ebook EAN: 9782808001786

Paperback EAN: 9782808001793

Legal Deposit: D/2017/12603/610

Cover: © Primento

Digital conception by Primento, the digital partner of
publishers.